The 21st Century Guitar Method

GUITAR METHOD 1

by AARON STANG

Everyone who begins an instrument—whether a child, teenager, or adult—has one thing in common: they are excited and looking forward to an enjoyable new experience. This method has been designed to encourage that enthusiasm by providing a carefully thought-out, musical, and fun way to learn. The musical examples represent all styles from folk to rock, reflecting the diverse interests of most guitarists. Tablature is used as an aid in learning new material, and suggested accompaniment parts have been included, enabling the teacher to play along and making the lesson more enjoyable for all (accompaniment parts are included on the accompanying recording as well). If you're learning on your own, the included recording will be invaluable; always learn what something sounds like before attempting to play it.

A Very Special Thanks

...to my wife, Audrey, for her unswerving support,
...to Sandy Feldstein, without whose suggestions and guidance this book would not have been possible,
...to Dan Warner for contributing his talent to the project,
...to Richard Hoover of the Santa Cruz Guitar Company and Tom Anderson of Tom Anderson Guitars for the use of their amazing instruments.

This book is dedicated to my daughter, Kelsey Rae.
Photography: Robert Santos
Recording: Ray Lyon, Aaron Stang and Dan Warner

Copyright © MMV by Alfred Publishing Co., Inc.
All rights reserved. Printed in USA.

ISBN-10: 0-89898-727-X (Book)
ISBN-13: 978-0-89898-727-0 (Book)
ISBN-10: 0-89898-729-6 (Book & CD)
ISBN-13: 978-0-89898-729-4 (Book & CD)

- CONTENTS -

CONTENTS

Two-String Rock

Ode to Joy

6

7

The Guitar

Electric

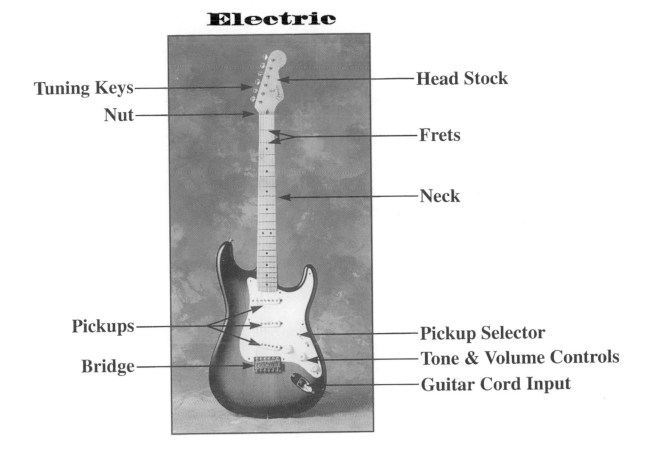

Tuning Keys ——— Head Stock

Nut ———

Frets

Neck

Pickups ———

Pickup Selector

Bridge ———

Tone & Volume Controls

Guitar Cord Input

Steel String Acoustic

Although any guitar can be used for virtually any kind of music, the **electric guitar** is most commonly used in popular music (Rock, Country, Jazz, etc.), especially when playing with a band. The electric guitar is usually played with a pick.

The **steel string guitar** is perfect for strumming and accompanying yourself. It can be played with a pick or finger-style.

The **nylon string guitar** is almost always played with the fingers and is ideal for solo and classical guitar styles.

Nylon String Acoustic

Technique

The pick should be held firmly between the thumb and index finger.

The thumb should be placed behind the neck. The fingers should be placed right behind the frets, not on top of, or in between them.

Sitting Position

Classic Position

Standing Position

Tuning The Guitar

Electronic Tuners:

Many brands of small, battery operated tuners, similar to the one shown below, are available. Simply follow the instructions supplied with your tuner.

Tuning the Guitar to a piano:

One of the easiest ways to tune a guitar is to a piano keyboard. The six strings of the guitar are tuned to the keyboard notes shown in the following diagram:

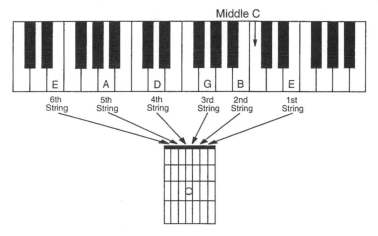

Tuning the Guitar to Itself (Relative Tuning):

1. Tune the 6th string to *E* on the piano (or some other fixed pitch instrument). You can also use a pitch pipe or an electronic guitar tuner.

2. Depress the 6th string at the 5th fret. Play it and you will hear the note *A*, which is the same note as the 5th string open. Turn the 5th string turning key until the pitch of the 5th string matches that of the 6th string.

3. Depress the 5th string at the 5th fret. Play it and you will hear the note *D*, which is the same note as the 4th string open. Turn the 4th string tuning key until the pitch of the 4th string matches that of the 5th string.

4. Depress the 4th string at the 5th fret. Play it and you will hear the note *G*, which is the same note as the 3rd string open. Turn the 3rd string tuning key until the pitch of the 3rd string matches that of the 4th string.

5. Depress the 3rd string at the 4th fret. Play it and you will hear the note *B*, which is the same note as the 2nd string open. Turn the 2nd string tuning key until the pitch of the 2nd string matches that of the 3rd string.

6. Depress the 2nd string at the 5th fret. Play it and you will hear the note *E*, which is the same note as the 1st string open. Turn the 1st string tuning key until the pitch of the 1st string matches that of the 2nd string.

Music Notation

There are seven natural notes. They are named for the first seven letters of the alphabet: A B C D E F G. After G, we begin again with A.

Music is written on a **staff**. The staff consists of five lines with four spaces between the lines:

At the beginning of the staff is a treble or G clef. (The treble clef is known as the G clef because it encircles the 2nd line G.) The clef determines the location of notes on the staff. All guitar music is written on a treble clef.

The notes are written on the staff in alphabetical order. The first line is E:

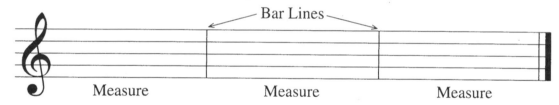

Notes can extend above, and below, the treble clef. When they do, **ledger lines** are added. Following is the approximate range of the guitar from the lowest note, open sixth string "E," to "B" on the first string, 17th fret.

The staff is divided into *measures* by *bar lines*. A heavy double bar line marks the end of the music:

Tablature is a type of music notation that is specific to the guitar; its use dates back to the 1600's. Tablature illustrates the location of notes on the neck of the guitar. Tablature is usually used in conjunction with a music staff. The notes and rhythms are indicated in the music staff; the tablature shows where those notes are played on the guitar.

The location of any note is indicated by the placement of fret numbers on the strings.

1st string
2nd string
3rd string
4th string
5th string
6th string

In this book, tablature will be used with all new notes and fingerings. "Tab" will also be used on all pop songs and as an aid to learning the more challenging arrangements; thereby making the learning process easier and more fun.

Rhythm Notation And Time Signatures

At the beginning of every song is a time signature. 4/4 is the most common time signature:

4 FOUR COUNTS TO A MEASURE
4 A QUARTER NOTE RECEIVES ONE COUNT

The top number tells you how many counts per measure.
The bottom number tells you which kind of note receives one count.

The time value of a note is determined by three things:

1) note head: o •

2) stem:

3) flag:

o This is a whole note. The note head is open and has no stem. In 4/4 time, a whole note receives 4 counts.

This is a half note. It has an open note head and a stem. A half note receives 2 counts.

This is a quarter note. It has a solid note head and a stem. A quarter note receives 1 count.

This is an eighth note. It has a solid note head and a stem with a flag attached. An eighth note receives 1/2 count.

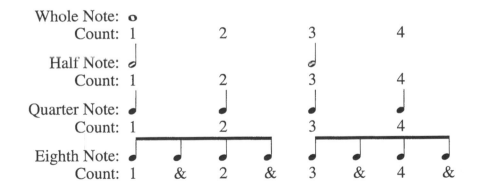

Whole Note: o			
Count: 1	2	3	4
Half Note:			
Count: 1	2	3	4
Quarter Note:			
Count: 1	2	3	4
Eighth Note:			
Count: 1 &	2 &	3 &	4 &

Count out loud and clap the rhythm to this excerpt from *Jingle Bells*.

Four Counts Per Measure

Jin - gle bells!   Jin - gle bells!   Jin - gle all the way!
1   2   3   4   1   2   3   4   1   2   3   4   1   2   3   4

A Quarter Note Receives One Count

The Notes on the First String

E Open	F First Finger First Fret	G Third Finger Third Fret

E (Open)　　　　　F (1st Fret)　　　　　G (3rd Fret)

Important:

A whole note gets 4 counts: **o** = 4 counts

A half note gets 2 counts: ♩ = 2 counts

A quarter note gets 1 count: ♩ = 1 count

Play all notes with a downstroke (⊓).
(Strike the string with a downward attack of the pick.)

1 Whole Notes:

Count: 1　2　3　4

Play slowly, with a steady beat.

2 Half Notes:

Count: 1　2　3　4

Say note names aloud.

3 Quarter Notes:

Count: 1　2　3　4

For more on note reading, theory and understanding the fretboard, see the *Theory Workshop* books of *Belwin's 21st Century Guitar Library*.

Note: Throughout the book, gray chord symbols are for teacher accompaniment.

Folk Song

A.S.

Suggested Teacher Accompaniment:

Flamenco Fantasy

A.S.

Always count with a steady beat—like the ticking of a clock.
Don't slow down, speed up or pause.

The Blues Beat

A.S.

Suggested Teacher Accompaniment:
(Shuffle feel)

For a complete rock guitar method, see the *Rock Shop* books of *Belwin's 21st Century Guitar Library.*

The Notes on the Second String:

B
Open

B (Open)

C
First Finger
First Fret

C (1st Fret)

D
Third Finger
Third Fret

D (3rd Fret)

1

Count: 1 2 3 4

2

Count: 1 2 3 4

3

Count: 1 2 3 4

String Combination Study:

Say notes aloud as you play.

For more on note reading, theory and understanding the fretboard, see the *Theory Workshop books* of *Belwin's 21st Century Guitar Library*.

Jingle Bells

J. Pierpont

Brightly

Jin - gle bells! Jin - gle bells! Jin - gle all the way! Oh, what fun it

is to ride a one - horse o - pen sleigh. ____ Jin - gle bells! Jin - gle bells!

Jin - gle all the way! Oh, what fun it is to ride a one-horse o - pen sleigh.

Aura Lee

Traditional American Folk Song

Slowly

As the black - bird in the spring, 'neath the wil - low tree,

sat and piped I heard him sing, sing of Au - ra Lee.

Suggested Teacher Accompaniment:
(Slowly)

The Boogie Shuffle

A.S.

Medium tempo

Suggested Teacher Accompaniment:
(Medium tempo - shuffle feel)

Tied Notes

A curved line connecting two notes of the same pitch is called a *tie*. Play the first note and hold it for the time value of both notes combined. Do not play the second note.

All Tied Up

Mary Ann

Caribbean

All day all night, Mar - y Ann, _____ down by the

sea - shore sift - ing sand. _____ All the lit - tle chil - dren love

Mar - y Ann, _____ down by the sea - shore sift - ing sand. _____

Power Rock

A.S.

Suggested Teacher Accompaniment:

(Straight-eighth rock)

14 Not all songs begin on beat 1. Many songs begin with an incomplete measure. *Notes played before the first complete measure are called **pick-up notes.*** The missing beats are usually found in the last measure of the song.

Pick-Up Piece and *When The Saints Go Marching In* both begin on the second beat of an incomplete measure. Count the missing beat (1) out loud and then begin playing on 2.

Pick-up Piece

When the Saints Go Marching In

The Notes on the Third String:

For more on note reading, theory and understanding the fretboard, see the *Theory Workshop* books of *Belwin's 21st Century Guitar Library*.

A dotted half note receives 3 counts: 𝅗𝅥. = 3 counts

Note: A dot adds half the value of the note it follows. Since a half note (𝅗𝅥) receives 2 counts, the dot is equal to 1 count. The half note and the dot combined equal 3 counts: 𝅗𝅥 +• = 3
(2) (1)

Oh, Susanna

Gently, a la James Taylor

Stephen C. Foster

I come from Al - a - bam - a with a ban - jo on my knee; I'm

goin' to Lou - 'si - an - a, my _____ true love for to see. It

rained all night the day I left, the weath - er it was dry. The

sun so hot I froze to death, Su - san - na don't you cry.

Oh, Su - san - na, oh, don't you cry for me. I

come from Al - a - bam - a with a ban - jo on my knee.

Suggested Teacher Accompaniment:

18 $\frac{3}{4}$ Three Counts to a Measure
A Quarter Note Receives One Count

Songs in 3/4 receive three counts per measure.

Down in the Valley

Kentucky Mountain Folk Song

We Three Kings of Orient Are

Christmas

Suggested Teacher Accompaniment:
(Moderately, with jazz waltz feel)

21 Repeat signs (:‖) tell us to play a section of music again. One backwards facing repeat sign means you should repeat to the beginning:

Repeat back to the beginning.

Red River Valley

Traditional Folk

Moderately

22

From this val - ley they say you are go - ing. _____ I will
Come and sit by my side if you love me. _____ Do not

miss your bright eyes and sweet smile, _____ for I
hast - en to bid me a - dieu; _____ but re -

know you are tak - ing the sun - shine _____ that has
mem - ber the Red Riv - er Val - ley, _____ and the

light - ed my path - way a - while. _____
one that has loved you so true. _____

In this next song, allow each note to continue to ring for the entire measure. Keep your fingers curved while playing the fretted notes so that they do not stop the other strings from ringing. Do not lift your fingers from the notes until absolutely necessary.

Singing Strings

A.S.

Moderately

23

hold --------┤   *hold --------┤*   *continue simile*

A
Fourth Finger
Fifth Fret

A (5th Fret)

24 The high A is played on the first string, at the fifth fret, with the fourth finger.

Ledger Lines are placed above or below the staff. The high A is placed on the first ledger line above the staff.

Danny Boy

Irish Folk Song

25 Slowly, with feeling

Oh, Dan - ny Boy, the pipes, the pipes are call - ing . . . ___ From glen to glen, and down the moun-tain side. _____ The sum-mer's gone, and all the ros - es fall - ing . . . ___ it's you, it's you must go and I must bide. _____

Originally a French operatic song, *Plaisir d'Amour* is so popular that it has passed on into the folk and popular music genres. The song was set to new lyrics and recorded by Elvis Presley as *Can't Help Falling In Love*. It became his 46th Top 40 hit.

Plaisir D'Amour

Jean-Paul Martini

26 Gently

Suggested Teacher Accompaniment:

(Gently)

Blue Eyes Crying In The Rain was Willie Nelson's first record to reach the Top 40. The song is a country ballad and should be played slowly, with feeling.

Note: Most printed music for rock and pop guitar includes tablature. In this book, tablature will be included with all pop songs and rock guitar examples.

Blue Eyes Crying in the Rain

Words and Music by Fred Rose

For more pop and rock songs, with complete play-along recordings, see the *Song Trax* books of *Belwin's 21st Century Guitar Library*.

The Notes on the Fourth String

For more on note reading, theory and understanding the fretboard, see the *Theory Workshop* books of *Belwin's 21st Century Guitar Library*.

Amazing Grace

Eighth Notes

31 This is an eighth note: ♪
Two eighth notes equal one quarter note: ♪ + ♪ = ♩

Single eighth notes are written like this: ♪
In groups of two or more, eighth notes are beamed together: ♫ ♫♫

Counting Eighth Notes: In 4/4 time, each measure is divided into four equal beats. Eighth notes divide each beat in half. A beat can be divided in half by saying "and" in between each count.

1 & 2 & 3 & 4 &

The Down-Upstroke: The down-upstroke is one continuous movement—a note is played with a downstroke, then the next note is played with an upstroke *as the pick returns to playing position.* The pick hand should swing freely from the wrist in a slight arc.

Eighth notes are played with alternating down-upstrokes. Down on the counts (1 2 3 4) and up on "and."

Downstroke: ⊓
Upstroke: ∨

1 & 2 & 3 & 4 &

This next study is based on the rhythm to *Ten Little Indians*. Practice this until you feel comfortable with both the counting and down/up picking.

Eighth Note Picking Study:

Ten Little Indians

Folk Song

One lit-tle, two lit-tle, three lit-tle In-d'ans; four lit-tle, five lit-tle, six lit-tle In-d'ans;

sev-en lit-tle, eight lit-tle, nine lit-tle In-d'ans; ten lit-tle In-di-an boys.

Spy to Spy

Medium

A.S.

When a section of music falls between two repeat signs, repeat that section only:

Repeat only the section in between the repeat signs.

Take the repeat once, then continue on to the next section.

Formed in 1961, the Beach Boys are one of the most successful groups in Rock history. They originated the "California" sound with their four-part harmony, and fun, uptempo rock and roll songs about cars, girls and surfboards. *Surfin' Safari* was the Beach Boys' first hit single.

Surfin' Safari

Words and Music by
Brian Wilson and Mike Love

For more pop and rock songs, with complete play-along recordings, see the *Song Trax* books of *Belwin's 21st Century Guitar Library*.

A sharp sign (♯) raises the pitch of a note one-half step, a distance of one fret. When a sharp sign is indicated before a note, that note remains sharp for the rest of the measure. The sharp sign is cancelled at the bar line, unless tied.

F♯
Fourth Finger
Fourth Fret

F# (4th Fret)

F♯
Second Finger
Second Fret

F# (2nd Fret)

Earlier, on page 11, we played the first half of *Aura Lee*. Here is the complete version, placed in a different key.

Written in 1861, *Aura Lee* became a favorite of soldiers during the Civil War. The song has such a beautiful melody that, like *Plaisir d'Amour,* it was adapted and recorded by Elvis Presley. This new version of *Aura Lee* became the title song from Elvis' first movie—*Love Me Tender.*

Aura Lee

Civil War Era Folk Song

Slowly

As the black-bird in the spring, 'neath the wil-low tree. Sat and piped I heard him sing, sing of Au-ra Lee. Au-ra Lee, Au-ra Lee, maid of gold-en hair; sun-shine came a-long with thee and swal-lows in the air.

Suggested Teacher Accompaniment:

Key Signatures

37 Rather than placing a sharp sign before every F, the F♯ can be indicated at the beginning of the line. The sharp sign will be placed on the top line (where the F is written). This is called a **key signature,** and indicates that every F in the song is sharp.

Golden Slippers

Key Signature *(all F's are sharp)*

American Folk Song

Lively

38

Simple Gifts

Shaker Hymn

Moderate tempo

39

'Tis the gift to be sim-ple, 'tis the gift to be free, 'tis the

gift to come down where we ought to be, and when we find our-selves in the

place just ___ right 'twill ___ be in the val - ley of love and de - light.

Suggested Teacher Accompaniment:

(Moderate tempo)

The C, G and G7 Chords

A chord consists of two or more notes played at the same time. The C, G and G7 chords can all be played on the first four strings.

Chord Frame Diagrams are similar to tablature. They illustrate how chords are fingered on the guitar fretboard:

Chord Study:

The next example shows how you can create a good guitar part by holding down a chord and picking each note separately. Use all downstrokes.

Folk-Rock Style

hold ---------| *hold* ------------------| *continue simile*

Chord Study:

Often the rhythm of the chord accompaniment is indicated by **rhythm slashes.** The rhythm slashes indicate the strumming pattern.

Rhythm Slashes: ♩ = ♩ = 1 count   ♩ = ♩ = 2 counts   o = o = 4 counts

In the next song, the accompaniment part is indicated by rhythm slashes placed above the melody. Learn both the accompaniment and melody parts.

New River Train

Medium tempo   G   *continue strum pattern*   D7   Traditional

I'm rid-ing on the new riv-er train.   I'm rid-ing on the new riv-er train.   It's the

same old __ train that brought me here. _____ It's soon gon-na car-ry me a-way.

*The **Fermata Sign** (⌢) tells you to hold the indicated note or chord beyond its normal duration.*

27

The "Blues" is the most common song form in rock music. The basic blues chord progression is 12 bars long and is built on three chords. In the key of G these three chords are: G, C and D. Often 7th chords are used: G7, C7 and D7.

The three chords in a 12-bar blues are called the I (G), IV (C) and V (D) chords. The blues chord progression always follows the same basic form (with many possible variations):

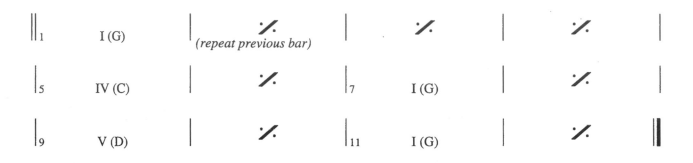

This next song combines single notes and chords to get the feel and sound of a rock/blues progression. Use all downstrokes for a solid, driving rhythm.

Natural Signs (♮): Notice the natural sign next to the F in bar 4. A natural sign cancels a sharp or flat for the rest of the measure.

Blues Changes

The feel of this next song is straight-ahead Rock and Roll and was first popularized by Chuck Berry. The single note lines are typical of what both the bass player and the guitarist might play on this type of song. This basic pattern continues to be the foundation of many new rock tunes.

Notice the use of the IV chord (C), instead of the V chord (D) in bar 10. This is the most common variation on the basic 12-bar blues progression.

The Notes on the Fifth String

A
Open

B
Second Finger
Second Fret

C
Third Finger
Third Fret

A (Open)   B (2nd Fret)   C (3rd Fret)

String Combination Study:

Say notes aloud as you play.

For more on note reading, theory and understanding the fretboard, see the *Theory Workshop* books of *Belwin's 21st Century Guitar Library*.

Cielito Lindo

The C, A Minor and D Minor Chords

So far you have been playing the C chord on four strings. Here is the full five string form of the C chord. The A minor chord is also a five-string chord form. The D minor chord uses four strings.

Fingering Tip: When moving from C to Am, keep your first and second fingers in place. Just shift your third finger. When moving from Dm to G7, keep your first finger in place and lift your second and third fingers.

Chord Study:

The Roots of Rock consists mostly of chords played one note at a time. This is called "arpeggio style." Hold each chord down for a full measure. Do not finger each note separately.

Glide Picking: Instead of alternate picking, allow the pick to glide from string to string as shown (all down strokes). For guitar parts like this, glide picking is easier and sounds smoother than alternate picking.

The Roots of Rock

52 This next song uses an eighth note rhythm to make the strum pattern more interesting. Use an upstroke to strum on "and."

Important Tip: When strumming up and down, always swing your pick hand loosely from the wrist. The pick should pivot in a semi-circle, so that on the up stroke, the top three strings (E, B and G) are accentuated.

Wrist Rock

53

Battle of Aughrim

54

Rock Workshop 102: Power Chords

55 Power chords are the foundation of many blues, rock and metal tunes. Power chords are two-note chord voicings. They are perfect for hard-driving rhythm guitar parts and are often played in unison with the bass line to provide a "big" sound with lots of bottom. Power chords are notated by the letter name of the chord (its root) followed by a 5: A5, D5, etc.

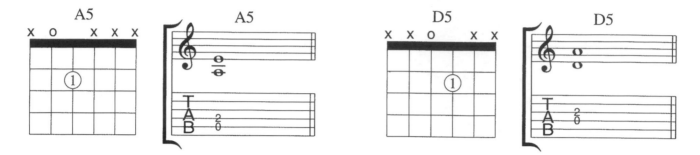

Notice that although A5 is played on the fifth and fourth strings and D5 is played on the fourth and third strings, they both look alike and are fingered alike—with the first finger at the second fret.

Power Study

56

Metalurgy shows how the 12-bar blues form has been adapted to Heavy Metal; the three chords are A5 (I), D5 (IV) and E5 (V)—more on E5 later. The song is a blues in "A" with a feel reminiscent of Anthrax and Iron Maiden.

First and Second Endings:

1st Ending | 2nd Ending

Repeat to the beginning

then skip to 2nd ending

Metalurgy

Hard rock feel

A.S.

For a complete rock guitar method, see the *Rock Shop* books of *Belwin's 21st Century Guitar Library*.

The Notes on the Sixth String:

E	F	G
Open	First Finger First Fret	Third Finger Third Fret

E (Open)   F (1st Fret)   G (3rd Fret)

Note: The notes on the sixth string are the same as on the first string—E, F and G.

String Combination Study:

Say notes aloud as you play.

For more on note reading, theory and understanding the fretboard, see the *Theory Workshop* books of *Belwin's 21st Century Guitar Library.*

Spanish Serenade

You've heard variations on this next guitar part hundreds of times, especially in the music of the early "surf" and Rockabilly guitarists, like The Venturas, Dick Dale, and Duane Eddy. The song is built on the 12-bar blues form (in E minor). To get a really authentic sound, use an electric guitar on the lead pickup *with lots of reverb.*

Surf-Rock Bass

Rock Workshop 103: Getting the Feel

61 Getting the right "feel" is everything when playing rock guitar. Two techniques that will help you get that feel are: **Accents** and **Palm Muting.**

Palm Mute: Gently lay the palm of your pick hand on the bridge of your guitar. If your hand is too far in front of the bridge, the strings will be too muted and not produce any tone at all. If your hand is too far behind the bridge, the strings will not be muted enough. The palm mute produces a short, muffled, percussive attack which greatly adds to the rhythmic drive and intensity of your playing.

The palm mute is indicated by the abbreviation: **P.M.**

The E5 Power Chord has its *root* on the sixth string. Notice that although each of the three power chords (E5, A5 and D5) are played on different string groups, they all look alike and are fingered alike—with the first finger at the second fret.

In the following three examples, work on getting a short, percussive attack on the muted chords. Note the contrast between the muted and unmuted sections.

Accents: An accent mark (>) tells you to emphasize a note or chord. The accents in this next example form a pattern which breaks the eight notes in each measure into three groups. You may want to try counting the pattern as shown, until you can "feel" it:

Muted rhythm with accents:

Rock Steady is a 12-bar blues in "A." The three chords are: A5 (I), D5 (IV) and E5 (V). Use the palm mute throughout and the accent pattern where indicated.

Rock Steady

For a complete rock guitar method, see the *Rock Shop* books of *Belwin's 21st Century Guitar Library*.

39

The Full G, G7 and E Minor Chords

Here are the complete, six string chord forms for G and G7, along with a new chord: E minor.

63 Notice how similar the G7 chord shape is to the C chord shape. To change between C and G7, simply move each finger to the next string.

To change between the G and D7 chords, slide your third finger along the first string while shifting your first and second fingers.

Chord Study 1:

Chord Study 2:

Loch Lomond

Scottish

64 **Medium tempo**

By ___ yon bon - nie banks, and by yon bon - nie braes, where the

(continue same strumming pattern)

sun shines bright on Loch Lo - mond, where me and my true love were

ev - er want to gae, on the bon - nie, bon - nie banks of Loch Lo - mond.

65 The sixth string F# is played at the second fret with the second finger:

F# (second fret)

The next song consists of two sections, labeled [A] and [B]. The song follows the form: A A B A. Many pop songs follow this same form. The [A] section is played arpeggio style. The [B] section changes to strumming style. This is the kind of rhythm guitar part you might play on a recording session for a soft rock ballad.

Rock Ballad

Six String Note Review:

Scarborough Fair

67

Gently

Traditional

Are you go-ing to Scar-bo-rough fair? _____ Pars-ly,
Have her make me a cam-bric shirt. _____ Pars-ly,

sage, rose-ma-ry and thyme. _____ Re-mem-ber me to
sage, rose-ma-ry and thyme. _____ With-out a seam or

one who lives there, _____ she once was a true love of mine.
fine need-le work, _____ then she'll be a true love of mine.

Suggested Teacher Accompaniment:

This next song is played arpeggio style. Tablature and chord frames have been included to help with the fingerings.

On Cloud Nine

Rock ballad

A.S.

On Cloud Nine (Teacher's Part)

(Rock ballad)

69 A rest is a period of silence. Each type of note has a corresponding rest:

Whole Rest: ▬ = o = 4 beats   Half Rest: ▬ = ♩ = 2 beats

Quarter Rest: 𝄽 = ♩ = 1 beat   Eighth Rest: 𝄾 = ♪ = 1/2 beat

When playing a note followed by a rest you should stop that note from ringing. To stop a fretted note from ringing, release the finger pressure on that note. To stop an open string from ringing, you can either gently touch the string with your left hand, or use the palm of your right hand to deaden the note.

Count out loud and tap your foot in the following studies.

Rest & Roll

70

Count the following exercise carefully. Move your pick in a constant down-up motion. When no note is played on the downbeat move your pick down anyway—only miss the string. This will put your hand in position to play the next note with an upstroke.

Eighth Rest Etude

71

This excerpt from *A Little Night Music* utilizes both the quarter and eighth note rests. Count carefully and tap your foot on each beat. (The foot should go down on beats 1, 2, 3 and 4 and up on "and.")

A Little Night Music

Wolfgang Amadeus Mozart

72

The blues boogie pattern is based on alternating between the basic two-note power chord and a two-note sixth chord:

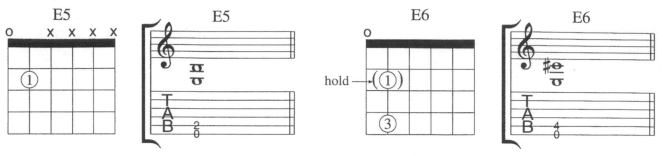

When changing from E5 to E6, keep your first finger on the B as you place your third finger on the C♯. Note: C♯ is at the fourth fret, one fret above C.

Now try alternating between A5 and A6. When changing from A5 to A6, keep your first finger on E as you place your third finger on F♯:

Now alternate between D5 and D6. When changing from D5 to D6, keep your first finger on A as you place your third finger on B. *Notice that you are now playing B on the third string (fourth fret) instead of the second string (open).* On the guitar, most notes can be played in more than one location.

Notice that when alternating E5/E6, A5/A6 and D5/D6 the fingering pattern remains the same—even though each is played on a different string group.

Now, let's combine the three patterns into a 12-bar blues. You've heard this pattern in the songs of Chuck Berry, the Beatles, the Stones, Clapton, Stevie Ray Vaughan, Van Halen and just about every band that's ever played rock.

The Boogie Progression

For a complete rock guitar method, see the *Rock Shop* books of *Belwin's 21st Century Guitar Library.*

Everything you've studied so far comes together in *Old Time Rock & Roll.* Note that the rhythm guitar part is based on an 8-bar version of the basic boogie progression studied in Rock Workshop 104:

The C# found in measures 2 and 6 is located one fret above C: second string, second fret. (The small size notes and tab numbers [called cue size] indicate variations on the melody in the second and third verses.)

Old Time Rock & Roll

Words and Music by
GEORGE JACKSON and
THOMAS E. JONES III

For more pop and rock songs, with complete play-along recordings, see the *Song Trax* books of *Belwin's 21st Century Guitar Library.*

Chorus:
w/Rhy. Fig. 1 (Rhythm Guitar)

Verse 2:
Don't try to take me to a disco,
You'll never even get me out on the floor.
In ten minutes I'll be late for the door,
I like that old time a rock and roll.
(To Chorus:)

Verse 3:
Won't go to hear 'em play a tango.
I'd rather hear some blues or funky old soul.
There's only one sure way to get me to go,
Start playing old time rock and roll.

Verse 4:
Call me a relic, call me what you will,
Say I'm old-fashioned, say I'm over the hill.
Today's music ain't got the same soul.
I like that old time rock and roll.
(To Chorus:)

Guitar Chord Chart

The following chart shows all of the most commonly used guitar chords.
o indicates an open string. x indicates the string is not to be played.